The All About Series

All About ... Canadian Sports

Soccer

Barb McDermott and Gail McKeown
Reidmore Books

Reidmore Books Inc.

For more information contact
Nelson Thomson Learning,
1120 Birchmount Road,
Scarborough, Ontario,
M1K 5G4.
Or you can visit our
internet site at
http://www.nelson.com

Printed and bound in Canada
2 3 4 5   03 02 01 00

We acknowledge the financial support of the
Government of Canada through the
Book Publishing Industry Development Program (BPIDP)
for our publishing activities.

Canadä

Canadian Cataloguing in Publication Data
McDermott, Barb.
All about Canadian sports : soccer

(All about series)
Includes index.
ISBN 1-896132-57-X

1. Soccer—Canada—Juvenile literature. I. McKeown, Gail. II. Title.
III. Series: McDermott, Barb. All about series.
GV944.C3M32 1999   j796.334'0971   C99-910778-X

About the Authors

Barb McDermott and Gail McKeown are highly experienced
kindergarten teachers living in Ontario. Both hold Bachelor of Arts and
Bachelor of Education degrees, Early Childhood diplomas, specialist
certificates in Primary Education, and have completed qualification
courses in Special Education. As well, Gail has a specialist certificate in
Reading and Visual Arts, and Barb has one in Guidance.

Content Reviewer

James Lloyd Mandigo, Faculty of Physical Education and Recreation,
University of Alberta

Sports Historian

Dr. PearlAnn Reichwein, Assistant Professor, Faculty of Physical Education
and Recreation, University of Alberta

Credits

Editorial: Leah-Ann Lymer, Scott Woodley, David Strand
Illustration, design and layout: Bruno Enderlin, Leslieanna Blackner Au
Diagram on page 13: Wendy Johnson, Johnson Cartographics

Photo Credits

Cover photo: Alberta Soccer
Association/George Sport Photo
Stamp photo: Alberta Soccer
Association/Westway Photo

Page

1 Dale Macmillan
3 Alberta Soccer
Association/Westway Photo
5 Les Jones/Covershots
7 Les Jones/Covershots
9 Alberta Soccer Association/George
Sport Photo
11 Alberta Soccer
Association/Westway Photo
15 Dale Macmillan
17 Dale Macmillan
19 Department of Athletics,
University of Alberta
21 Alberta Soccer
Association/Westway Photo
23 Dale Macmillan
25 Dale Macmillan
27 Alberta Soccer Association/
George Sport Photo

We have made every effort to
identify and credit the sources of
all photographs, illustrations, and
information used in this textbook.
Reidmore Books appreciates any
further information or corrections;
acknowledgment will be given in
subsequent editions.

Table of Contents
(All about what's in the book)

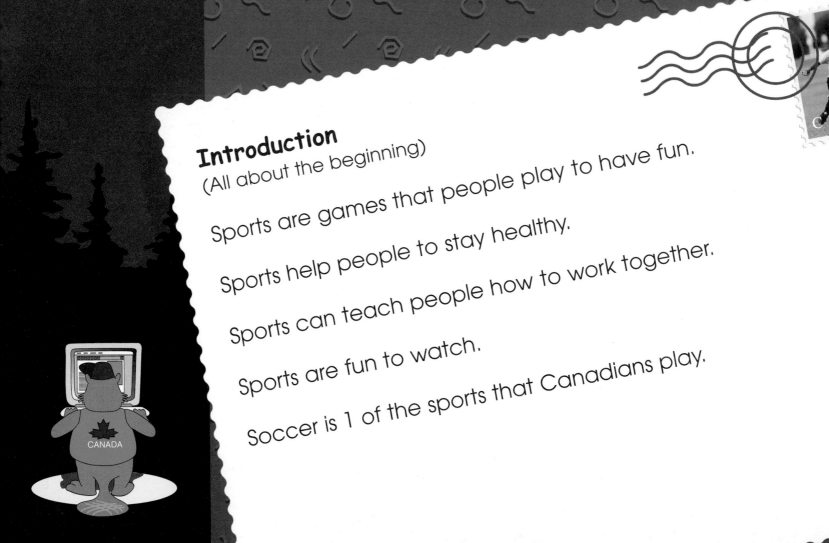

Introduction
(All about the beginning)

Sports are games that people play to have fun.

Sports help people to stay healthy.

Sports can teach people how to work together.

Sports are fun to watch.

Soccer is 1 of the sports that Canadians play.

Soccer Is a Fun Sport

Introduction
(All about soccer)

Soccer is a game played between 2 teams.

Soccer is usually played outdoors on a grass field.

Soccer players wear special **uniforms.**

Soccer is played with a special ball.

Soccer players use their feet, their head, and their body to get the ball into the other team's net.

Soccer Is Played Outdoors

History
(All about how soccer began)

The **ancient** Chinese and Romans 1st played games that were like soccer 1000s of years ago.

Soccer came to England in the 1800s and was 1st called football.

Soccer is still called football in **Europe.**

The 1st rules for soccer were written in 1848.

The **British** brought soccer with them when they moved to other places around the world.

British and Canadian Soccer Teams in 1888

History
(All about how soccer began)

The 1st organized soccer game in Canada was played in Toronto, Ontario in 1859.

The Dominion Football **Association** was formed in Montreal, Quebec in 1878.

The Dominion Football Association was later called the Canadian Soccer Association.

The Canadian Soccer Association teaches people how to play the sport and gives awards to soccer players and **coaches.**

A Soccer Team in Alberta in 1905

Uniform

(All about what soccer players wear)

Soccer players wear **jerseys** and shorts.

Soccer players wear pads under thick socks below their knees.

Soccer players wear the pads to help **protect** their legs against kicks from other players.

Goalkeepers wear padded gloves that help them to grip the ball.

Soccer players wear special shoes that help them to grip the grass field.

Soccer Players Wear Special Shoes

Equipment
(All about what is used to play soccer)

Soccer is played with a soccer ball, which is hollow.

The ball is filled with air so that it can bounce.

The ball is made from leather.

The ball is often white or black and white.

The ball is about 22 cm in **diameter** and weighs about 400 g.

Soccer Balls Are Filled with Air

Facility
(All about where soccer is played)

Soccer is played on a flat, rectangle-shaped field of grass.

The field can be 91 to 100 m long and 64 to 73 m wide.

The field is painted with touchlines on the sides and goal lines at the ends.

The field is painted with other lines that show the middle of the field and the goalkeepers' areas.

Each net is in the middle of each goal line, and is 7 m wide and 2 m high.

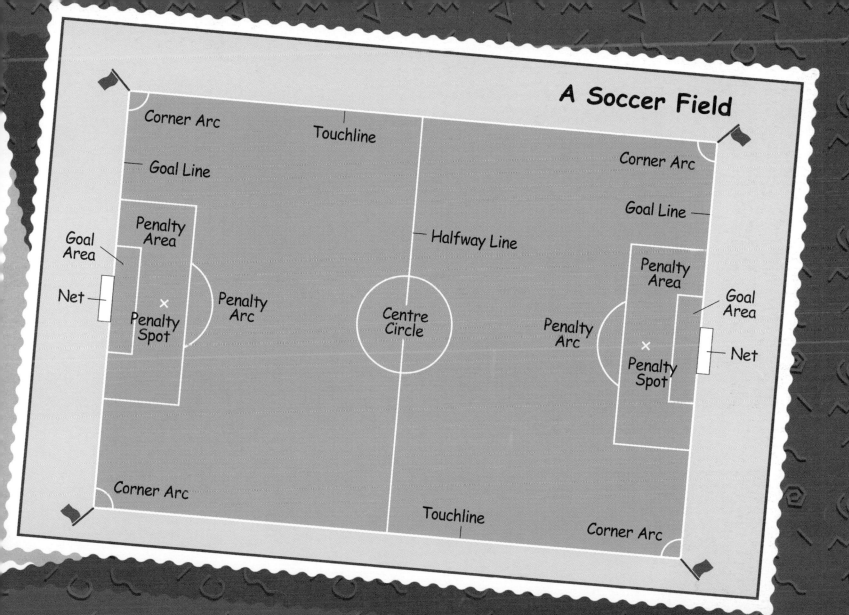

A Soccer Field

Corner Arc

Touchline

Goal Line

Corner Arc

Goal Line

Penalty Area

Goal Area

Halfway Line

Net

Penalty Spot

Penalty Arc

Penalty Area

Centre Circle

Goal Area

Penalty Arc

Net

Penalty Spot

Corner Arc

Touchline

Corner Arc

Teams
(All about the players)

Soccer has 11 players on each team.

Each team has defenders, midfielders, and forwards.

These players pass the ball to each other and move it closer to the other team's net.

Each team has specialists, who are players with special jobs.

One of the specialists is the goalkeeper, who tries to keep the ball out of his or her team's net.

Soccer Teams Have 11 Players

Rules
(All about how soccer is played)

A soccer game lasts for 90 minutes.

The 90 minutes are divided into 2 halves that last 45 minutes each.

The team that has the ball is called the offensive team.

The team that does not have the ball is called the defensive team.

The Team with the Ball Is the Offensive Team

Rules
(All about how soccer is played)

The referee flips a coin before the game begins.

The team that wins the coin flip can choose which side of the field they want to play on.

The game starts when a player kicks the ball from centre to a team member.

The offensive team tries to move the ball towards the defensive team's net.

The defensive team tries to stop the offensive team from moving the ball towards their net.

Each Player Tries to Kick the Ball to Her Team

Rules
(All about how soccer is played)

If 1 team scores a goal, the other team starts the game again at centre with a kick off.

The ball must completely cross the goal line at the net for a team to score.

Soccer players are allowed to touch the ball with any part of their bodies except their hands.

Goalkeepers can touch the ball with their hands.

Soccer has a referee, who makes sure the players follow the rules.

Goalkeepers Can Use Their Hands

Rules
(All about how soccer is played)

If the offensive team kicks the ball past the goal line but not into the net, then the defensive team gets a **goal kick.**

If the defensive team kicks the ball past the goal line but not into the net, then the offensive team gets a **corner kick.**

Many goals are scored from corner kicks.

If 1 team kicks the ball past the touchline, then the other team gets a **throw-in.**

Canada

A Throw-In

Skills
(All about what soccer teaches)

Soccer players learn to work with other members of their team.

Soccer players learn to watch the ball and move their bodies in response.

Soccer players learn how to run quickly so that they can move the ball past the other team.

Soccer players learn how to kick the ball so that they can try to score goals.

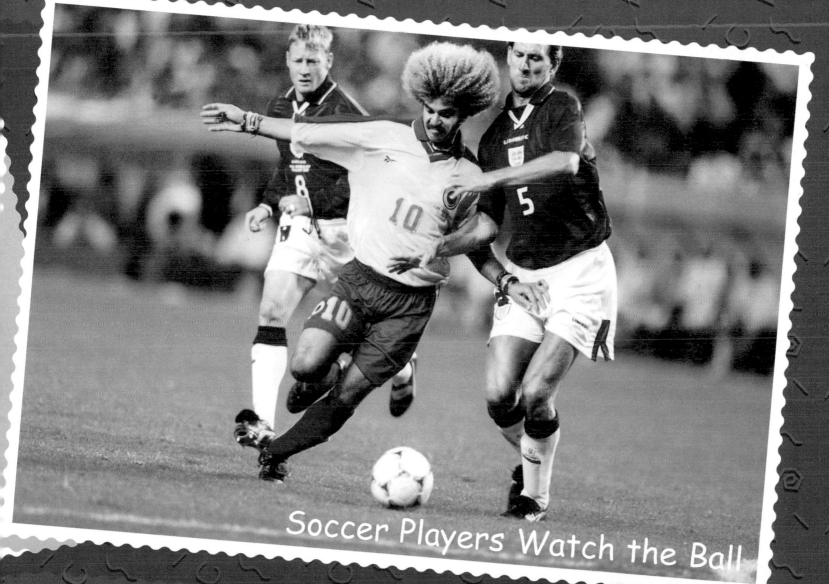

Soccer Players Watch the Ball

Summary
(All about the ending)

Soccer is a game that Canadians play to have fun and stay healthy.

Soccer came from ancient China and Rome.

Soccer is a game in which 2 teams try to kick a ball into each other's net.

Soccer is an amazing sport ... enjoyed by Canadians!

CANADA

Soccer Is an Amazing Sport

Glossary
(All about what the words mean)

ancient (page 4)
Ancient means very old and no longer present.

association (page 6)
An association is a group of people who are joined together for a common purpose.

British (page 4)
British means from Britain. Britain is a country made up of England, Scotland, Wales, and Northern Ireland.

coaches (page 6)
A coach is a person who teaches or trains a sports team.

corner kick (page 22)
When the ball is moved over the goal line by the defensive team, then the offensive team gets to kick the ball into the play area from the corner of the field. This is called a corner kick.

diameter (page 10)
Diameter is how wide a circle is. To measure how wide a circle is, draw a line from 1 side of the circle to the other and measure the line. The line must go through the centre of the circle.

Europe (page 4)
Europe is an area that includes the countries of France, Italy, Germany, Poland, and the Czech Republic.

goal kick (page 22)
When the ball is moved over the goal line by the offensive team, then the defensive team is allowed to kick the ball from inside the goal area. This is called a goal kick.

jerseys (page 8)
A jersey is a special kind of shirt.

protect (page 8)
To protect something is to defend it from harm.

throw-in (page 22)
When the ball passes over a touchline, then the team which did not touch the ball last is given a throw-in. The player given a throw-in must keep both feet on the ground and throw the ball with both hands.

uniforms (page 2)
A uniform is a special set of clothes that shows that a person plays a certain sport or has a certain job.